Building Washington, D.C.

Measuring the Area of Rectangular Shapes

Barbara M. Linde

PowerMath™

The Rosen Publishing Group's
PowerKids Press™
New York

Published in 2004 by The Rosen Publishing Group, Inc.
29 East 21st Street, New York, NY 10010

Book Design: Haley Wilson

Photo Credits: Cover © Mark Segal/Index Stock; pp. 4–5 © Matthew Borkoski/Index Stock; pp. 6–7 (map),
8–9 © Library of Congress; pp. 6 (George Washington), 11 (Banneker), 17, 22 (inset of Supreme Court
chamber) © Bettmann/Corbis; pp. 11, 20 by Maura B. McConnell; p. 13 © Corbis; pp. 14–15 (White
House) © Henry Kaiser; pp. 18–19 (Capitol building) © Wendell Metzen/Index Stock; pp. 18–19 (Rotunda)
© David Wasserman/Index Stock; pp. 22–23 (Supreme Court building) © William Holdman/Index Stock;
p. 24 © Jim Tuten/Index Stock; p. 26 © Bob Burch/Index Stock; p. 28 © Maps.com/Index Stock.

Library of Congress Cataloging-in-Publication Data

Linde, Barbara M.
  Building Washington, D.C. : measuring the area of rectangular shapes /
Barbara M. Linde.
      p. cm. — (PowerMath)
Includes index.
  ISBN 0-8239-8980-1 (lib. bdg.)
  ISBN 0-8239-8867-8 (pbk.)
  6-pack ISBN: 0-8239-7375-1
1. Rectangle—Juvenile literature. 2. Area measurement—Juvenile
literature. 3. Washington (D.C.)—Buildings, structures, etc—Juvenile
literature. I. Title. II. Series.
  QA482 .L65 2004
  516.2—dc21
                            2002156677

Manufactured in the United States of America

Contents

The New Federal City

Area is the number of square **units** inside a shape. For example, when you are using yards to measure the area of a shape, you are looking for the number of 1-yard-by-1-yard squares it takes to fill the shape. This unit is known as a square yard.

To find the area of a rectangle or square, multiply the length of the shape by the width. The **formula** for this is: area equals length times width, or $a = l \times w$. If you know a plot of land is 5 yards in length and 5 yards in width, you can find the area. Multiply 5 by 5 to get 25 square yards.

People in many types of work need to know the areas of spaces. For example, builders need to know the area of a plot of land before they can plan the size and location of buildings and streets. Builders used the formula $a = l \times w$ to plan our nation's capital city, Washington, D.C.

5 Yards

5 Yards

Today, Washington, D.C., is a busy place. About 200 years ago, there was no Washington, D.C. Instead of a city, there were marshes, forests, and farms. The only nearby communities were Alexandria and Georgetown.

Do the Math

$$\begin{array}{r} 5 \text{ yards} \\ \times\ 5 \text{ yards} \\ \hline 25 \text{ square} \\ \text{yards} \end{array}$$

George Washington

Before 1789, U.S. government business was done mostly in New York and Philadelphia. Congress wanted one special place for the national government. Congress said the new federal district should be a square that was 10 miles on each side. This was to be called the District of Columbia. It would not be a part of any state. The capital city of Washington would be inside the district.

President George Washington chose the plot of land. It was near the middle of the original 13 states. The Potomac and Anacostia Rivers flowed through the area. These rivers would provide water and **transportation**. Part of the land that Washington wanted belonged to the state of Virginia, and part of it belonged to Maryland. These 2 states each gave up some of their land to create the nation's new capital.

The original District of Columbia was a square that was 10 miles on each side. To find the area, multiply 10 miles by 10 miles to get 100 square miles.

Do the Math

$$
\begin{array}{r}
10 \text{ miles} \\
\times\ 10 \text{ miles} \\
\hline
00 \\
+10 \\
\hline
100 \text{ square miles}
\end{array}
$$

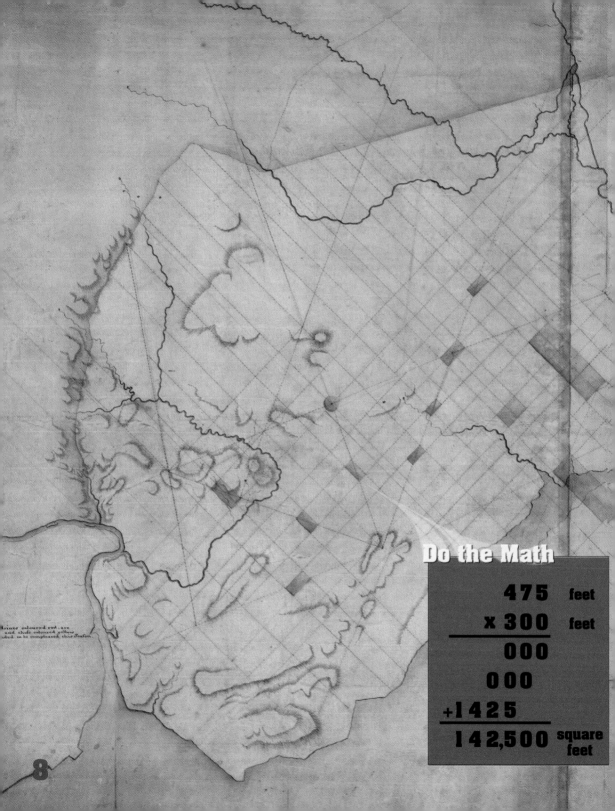

Do the Math

475	feet
x 300	feet
000	
000	
+1425	
142,500	square feet

8

The Survey Team

Before any buildings could be constructed, the land had to be **surveyed**. The exact boundaries for the District of Columbia had to be found and marked. Careful records of the measurements had to be kept. A map of the land had to be made. This work would take months. Since the measurements had to be exact, only a very skilled **surveyor** could do the job.

In 1791, President George Washington chose Andrew Ellicott to conduct the survey for the new federal city. Ellicott was a well-known surveyor and **engineer** from Maryland. He had already done survey work for Virginia, Pennsylvania, Georgia, and North Carolina.

Ellicott knew an African American surveyor named Benjamin Banneker. Ellicott was impressed with Banneker's knowledge of math and science, so he hired Banneker for the survey team.

This map from 1791 shows one idea for public parks in the new capital. If a park has a length of 457 feet and a width of 300 feet, what is the area? To find out, multiply 457 by 300 to get 142,500 square feet.

Benjamin Banneker was a free man, not a slave like most African Americans of the time. Banneker could read and write, and he had taught himself math and science. He used these skills to teach himself how to survey land. Joining the survey team was exciting for him. He was 60 years old and had never been more than 12 miles away from his home. Now he would travel about 40 miles to help plan the nation's capital city.

The surveyors worked outside and slept in tents all winter. Banneker took measurements, cared for the equipment, and kept records. In the spring, Banneker went home because he was sick. The work he had done was used by the rest of the survey team.

Banneker became known as the first African American man of science. There is a park in Washington, D.C., named in his honor. The park is shaped like a circle, and is southwest of the Capitol building.

The street near Benjamin Banneker Park is about 880 feet long and 62 feet wide. To find the area of the street, multiply 880 feet by 62 feet to get 54,560 square feet.

Do the Math

880 feet
x 62 feet
─────
1 7 6 0
+5 2 8 0
─────
5 4,5 6 0 square feet

Benjamin Banneker

BENJAMIN
BANNEKER
PARK

President Washington chose Pierre L'Enfant (LAWN-fawnt) to design Washington, D.C. L'Enfant used Ellicott's survey information as he created his plan. L'Enfant wanted the capital to be a grand place. He put the Capitol and the White House on hills so they could easily be seen. He created wide streets and beautiful parks.

L'Enfant was asked to give a completed copy of his plan to some officials. When he did not do this, he was fired. Andrew Ellicott took over as city planner. The design of Washington, D.C., became a combination of the ideas of both men.

The following pages describe some of the sites in Washington, D.C. As you read, think of the work that Ellicott, Banneker, L'Enfant, and others did to create the capital city.

One of the public walkways on L'Enfant's plan was about 52 feet long and 41 feet wide. To find the area, multiply 52 feet by 41 feet to get 2,132 square feet.

The Original Plan of Washington, D.C.
Drawn by Pierre L'Enfant, 1791

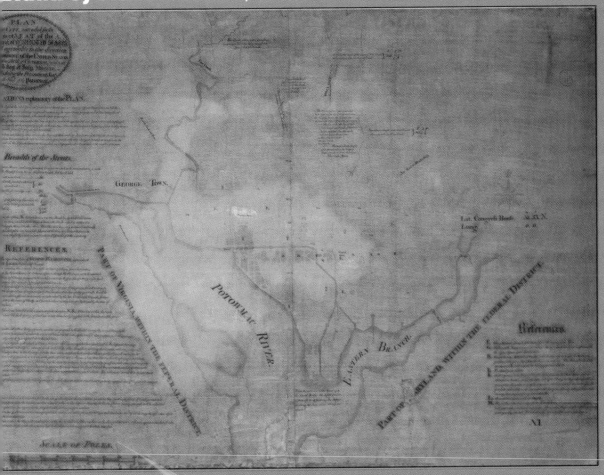

Do the Math

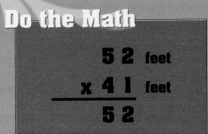

```
        5 2  feet
      x 4 1  feet
      ───────
        5 2
    + 2 0 8
    ───────
    2 , 1 3 2  square
               feet
```

The White House

The White House in Washington, D.C., is the home of the president of the United States. The White House also has offices for government officials. It is located at 1600 Pennsylvania Avenue NW (northwest). Built in 1792, the White House was the first building to be constructed in the new capital. Since it was not finished while George Washington was still president, he never lived there. However, the White House has been home to every other president.

Do the Math

$$
\begin{array}{r}
1\,6\,5 \text{ feet} \\
\times\quad 8\,5 \text{ feet} \\
\hline
8\,2\,5 \\
+\,1\,3\,2\,0 \\
\hline
1\,4{,}0\,2\,5 \text{ square feet}
\end{array}
$$

When it was built, the White House was the largest house in the United States. It measured about 165 feet long and 85 feet wide. To find the area, multiply 165 feet by 85 feet to get 14,025 square feet.

14

As the country grew, the number of government officials also grew. The White House became very crowded. In 1902, the West Wing was added. Government offices are in this part of the building. The president works in the Oval Office here. The president and his family live on the second floor in the East Wing. The East Wing is a private space, so tourists are not allowed to visit it.

Many of the rooms in the White House have names and special uses. The East Room is the biggest room in the White House. Today, the East Room is used for parties and other celebrations. Around 1800, President John Adams's wife, Abigail, hung the family's laundry in this room.

Can you imagine eating dinner in a room with about 140 people? You could do that if you were invited to the State Dining Room. You could enjoy a delicious meal prepared by chefs in the basement kitchen.

The president meets with the leaders of other countries in the Blue Room. President Grover Cleveland was married in this room in 1886. He is still the only president who was married in the White House.

A house could fit inside the East Room. It measures about 80 feet long and 37 feet wide. To find the area of the East Room, multiply 80 feet by 37 feet to get 2,960 square feet.

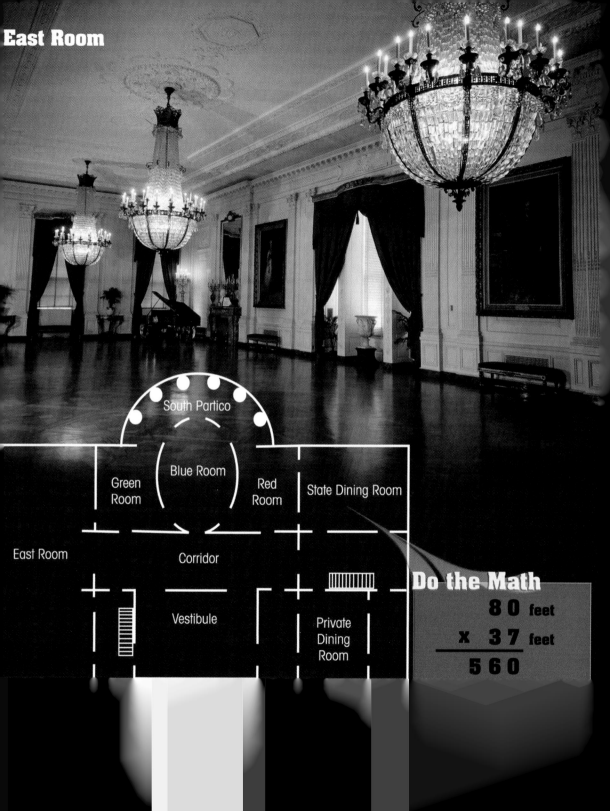

East Room

South Partico

Blue Room

Green
Room

Red
Room

State Dining Room

East Room

Corridor

Vestibule

Private
Dining
Room

Do the Math

```
    8 0 feet
x   3 7 feet
—————————
  5 6 0
```

Rotunda

```
      7 5 1  feet
  x 3 5 0  feet
  _____
      0 0 0
    3 7 5 5
 +2 2 5 3
 _____
  2 6 2,8 5 0  square
                feet
```

The Capitol building is 751 feet long and 350 feet wide. To find the area of the Capitol, multiply 751 feet by 350 feet to get 262,850 square feet.

The Capitol

The members of Congress meet in the Capitol and have offices in the building, too. The Capitol also houses a museum of American art and history. Millions of people from around the world visit the Capitol every year.

Construction of the Capitol building started in 1793. Over the next 200 years, several additions were made. Now the Capitol has about 550 rooms.

The Capitol **dome** is often shown as a symbol of our **democratic** form of government. The Statue of Freedom stands on top of the dome. The statue is taken down by helicopter when it needs to be cleaned.

The **Rotunda** is the part of the building under the dome. Here you can see historical paintings and statues of presidents.

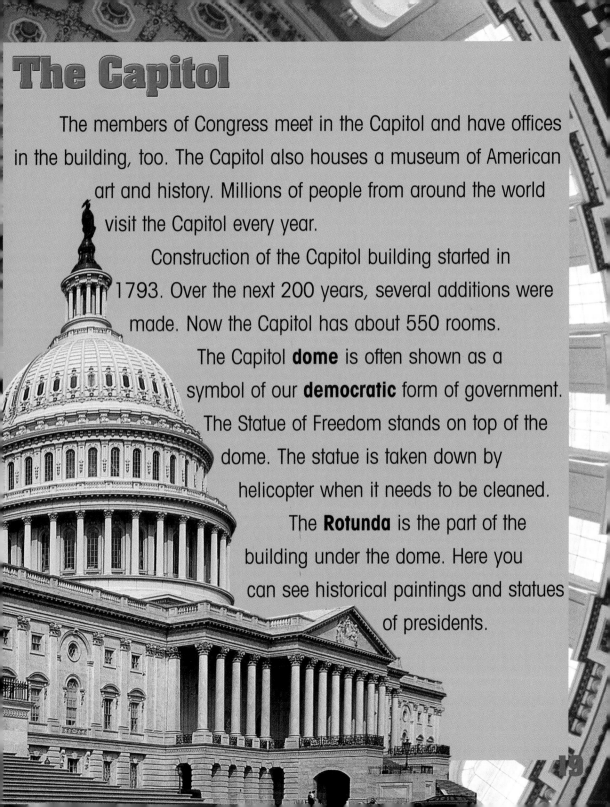

1 5 feet
x 1 5 feet
―――
7 5
+1 5
―――
2 2 5 square feet

Gatehouse

The Capitol gatehouses were built in 1829. Originally the Capitol had a fence around it. Gatehouses were placed in between sections of the fence. Guards stayed in the gatehouses while they were on duty. However, the sandstone used to build the gatehouses was not strong. Within about 50 years, the gatehouses could no longer be used. The fence was taken down. Two of the gatehouses were moved to Constitution Avenue at 15th Street and at 17th Street NW. Two others were moved to a park. If you look closely at the picture of the gatehouse shown here, you may see a dark line partway up the wall. This is a watermark. In times past, the Potomac River sometimes flooded. This mark shows how high the water rose.

Each gatehouse is a square that measures 15 feet on each side. What is the area of one gatehouse? To find out, multiply 15 feet by 15 feet to get 225 square feet.

$$
\begin{array}{r}
304 \\
385 \overline{)117{,}040} \\
-1155 \\
\hline
154 \\
-0 \\
\hline
1540 \\
-1540 \\
\hline
0
\end{array}
$$

The Supreme Court Building

The Supreme Court decides if the country's laws obey the Constitution. For the first 145 years after the Supreme Court was formed, its judges did not have a regular place to meet. They held court in other government buildings.

The Supreme Court building was constructed between 1932 and 1935. The two statues at the sides of the steps represent law and **justice**. The words above the entrance to the building say "Equal Justice Under Law."

Today you can watch the justices, or judges, as they hear cases. At the beginning of the case you'll hear a marshal say, "Oyez, oyez, oyez." This is French for "hear ye." The phrase lets everyone know that a Supreme Court justice is in the courtroom and ready to begin work.

The area of the Supreme Court building is 117,040 square feet. The length is 385 feet. If you know these two measurements, you can find the width. Divide the total area (117,040 square feet) by the length (385 feet) to get 304 feet.

Do the Math

$$
\begin{array}{r}
5\ 5 \text{ feet} \\
\times\ 5\ 5 \text{ feet} \\
\hline
2\ 7\ 5 \\
+\ 2\ 7\ 5 \\
\hline
3,0\ 2\ 5 \text{ square feet}
\end{array}
$$

The Washington Monument

The Washington Monument was built to honor the memory of America's first president—and the man who helped to build Washington, D.C.—George Washington. The Washington Monument is 555 feet 5 $\frac{1}{8}$ inches high. It's the tallest tower in the world that is made of stone. The shape of the monument is an **obelisk**. An obelisk is a column with 4 sides and a **pyramid** at the top.

The monument was started in 1848, but work stopped in 1854 when money ran short. When work started again in 1879, a slightly different shade of marble was used. You can see this change if you look closely. The monument was finished in 1884. It stands at the center of 4 other Washington, D.C., landmarks: the Capitol, the White House, the Jefferson **Memorial**, and the Lincoln Memorial.

People used to be able to walk up the 893 steps to the top. Now everyone must use the elevator. At the top you'll have a view of the whole capital region. When you come back down, you can look at the American flags around the base.

The square base of the monument is about 55 feet on each side. What is the area? To find out, multiply 55 feet by 55 feet to get 3,025 square feet.

$$
160 \overline{\smash{\big)}\ 3\,20,000} \quad \begin{array}{r} 2,000 \\ \end{array}
$$

$$
\begin{array}{r}
2,000 \\
160 \overline{\smash{\big)}\ 3\,20,000} \\
-3\,20 \\
\hline
0000 \\
\end{array}
$$

The Reflecting Pool is between the Lincoln Memorial and the Washington Monument. It is on a stretch of land called the Mall. If you stand at the Lincoln Memorial and look into the Reflecting Pool, you will see the upside-down image of the Washington Monument. If you stand at the Washington Monument and look toward the other end of the Reflecting Pool, you'll see the Lincoln Memorial.

The Reflecting Pool is only 3 feet deep. It takes 24 hours to fill the pool with water. People aren't allowed to swim or wade in the pool, but ducks often swim there. You can walk on the sidewalks or the grassy areas along the sides of the pool. It's fun to have a picnic under the shade trees. Many people say this is one of the most beautiful spots in the whole District of Columbia.

The area of the Reflecting Pool is 320,000 square feet. The width is 160 feet. If you know these two measurements, you can find the length. Divide the total area (320,000 square feet) by the width (160 feet) to get 2,000 feet.

Washington, D.C.

N

0   0.5 Mi

Wisconsin Ave

Glover Park

Georgetown

N St

M St

M St

L St

K St

K St

Washington Harbour

Foggy Bottom

West End

Dupont Circle

P St

Logan Circle

P St

O St

6th St

Rhode Island

N St

M St

9th St

5th St

New York Ave

Connecticut Ave

New Hampshire Ave

25th St

24th St

National Geographic

Massachusetts Ave

Franklin Park

12th St

Mt. Vernon Square

Washington Convention Center

K St

I St

Pennsylvania Ave

I (Eye) St

Theodore Roosevelt Memorial

Kennedy Center

George Washington University

Old Executive Offices

Lafayette Square

14th St

G St

13th St

11th St

Treasury Building

White House

F.B.I.

John Marshall Park

4th St

3rd St

2nd St

D St

E St

Virginia Ave

D.A.R.

O.A.S.

The Ellipse

Nat'l Aquarium

Constitution Ave

National Archives

C St

C St

Pennsylvania Ave

Roosevelt Bridge

GW Pkwy

Federal Reserve

Vietnam Veterans Memorial

Lincoln Memorial

Arlington Memorial Bridge

Reflecting Pool

West Potomac Park

Madison Dr

Washington Monument

The Mall

Jefferson Dr

D St

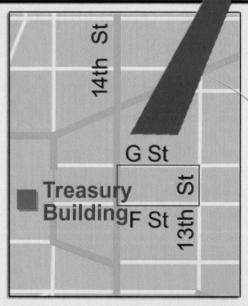

14th St

G St

Treasury Building

F St

13th St

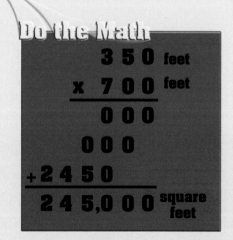

Do the Math

$$
\begin{array}{r}
3\ 5\ 0 \text{ feet} \\
\times\ 7\ 0\ 0 \text{ feet} \\
\hline
0\ 0\ 0 \\
0\ 0\ 0 \\
+\ 2\ 4\ 5\ 0 \\
\hline
2\ 4\ 5{,}0\ 0\ 0 \text{ square feet}
\end{array}
$$

Getting Around the City

There are hundreds of interesting things to see and do in Washington, D.C. You can walk through beautiful gardens, take a boat ride on the Potomac River, or visit war memorials. You could spend days in the wonderful museums. Many places of interest are on or near the Mall.

It's easy to walk or drive from place to place. The city is divided into 4 parts with the Capitol in the center. The streets that go from north to south have number names, such as 1st, 5th, or 21st. Streets that go from east to west have letter names, such as A, G, and M. Other streets cross at an angle. These are named for the states of the United States, such as Maryland, Virginia, and New York.

The block between 13th and 14th Streets NW and G and F Streets NW forms a rectangle. It is about 350 feet wide and 700 feet long. To find the area of the block, multiply 350 feet by 700 feet to get 245,000 square feet.

Area in Your Life

Surveyors aren't the only people who need to know how to find the area of a square or rectangle. This skill comes in handy all the time. Housepainters need to measure the area of a wall to know how much paint it will take to cover it. Carpenters need to measure the area of boards to make sure they have enough wood to make things like cabinets and dressers.

If you want a new rug in your bedroom, you'll want to buy a rug that fits. You will need to know the area of the room. If you want to put a garden in your yard, you'll need to know the area of the yard and the area of the garden that you want to make. Then you can buy the right amount of soil. From Washington, D.C., to your backyard, finding the area of squares and rectangles is an important part of life.

Glossary

democratic (deh-muh-KRA-tik) A word that describes a form of government under which all people are treated equally.

dome (DOHM) A rounded top on a building.

engineer (en-juh-NEAR) Someone trained in building things like roads and buildings.

formula (FOR-myuh-luh) A math rule that is written with numbers, letters, or symbols.

justice (JUHS-tuhs) Fairness.

memorial (muh-MOHR-ee-uhl) Something that is made to remind people of a person or event.

obelisk (AH-buh-lisk) A tall stone column with 4 sides that gets narrower as it rises and has a pyramid at the top.

pyramid (PEER-uh-mid) A solid figure with a square base and 4 triangular sides that meet in a point at the top.

rotunda (roh-TUHN-duh) A round room that may have a dome.

survey (SUHR-vay) To measure for size, shape, boundaries, etc. Also a plan or description of land.

surveyor (suhr-VAY-uhr) A person who measures land.

transportation (tranz-puhr-TAY-shun) The movement of people or goods.

unit (YOO-nit) A standard amount by which things are measured.

Index